Over 200

ENGLISH

IRREGULAR VERBS

Part 1

LEVELS

A1, A2, B1, B2, C1, C2

Over 200

ENGLISH

IRREGULAR VERBS

Part 1

LEVELS
A1, A2, B1, B2, C1, C2

DICTIONOPOLIS

YOUR FREE GIFT

As a way of saying thank you for your purchase, free flashcards for self-printing are available to readers of this book.

Enter the link below to your browser to get free instant access.

https://mailchi.mp/8ff48a0638e2/free-flashcards

CONTENTS

INTRODUCTION

Irregular verbs in the English language are common, and many of the first verbs you will learn are irregular. Learning these verbs early will help you to master the language quicker. This guide to the most common irregular verbs in English has each verb grouped by the Common European Framework of Reference for Languages (CEFR) level, making it a valuable resource for learning the language. We hope you find this book a valuable resource in your language journey and in building up your confidence in using English to communicate.

This guide uses the following format and conventions:

- The verb is displayed using the base form (infinitive - I), simple past (II), and the past participle (III).
- Each verb has a definition to make it easier to understand the context for the usage of the verb.

The following symbols are used in this guide.

The loudspeaker symbol means that you can hear the pronunciation of the word in all forms in the audiobook version (at the indicated time).

The star symbol signifies that the word in question occurs mainly in American English. When using the audiobook, you will hear the pronunciation of these words with this in both British and American.

☐ The card symbol with a number means the number of the flashcard. Remember to download the flashcards and use them systematically to speed up the memorizing process.

We believe that everyone can find something for themselves in our guide to irregular English verbs. For beginners, mastering irregular verbs will enhance your ability to learn English, and for advanced users, the guide is an essential aid in consolidating knowledge of irregular verbs.

We have put many hours of work into the preparation of this guide to irregular English verbs, and we hope you find this a valuable resource in supporting your language journey. We are always looking to improve our products to offer the best learning experience and would be grateful to hear your opinion and welcome your feedback. You can do this by clicking on the 'Write a customer review' button. We love to listen to our readers and read every review in person, so we look forward to hearing from you.

Thank you,

Dictionopolis Team

Special thanks to the following language consultants:

Alexandra Freeman
Joe Frost

With additional support from Jamie James.

LEVEL

A1

be

I be
bi

II was / were
wəz, wɒz / wə(r), wɜː(r)

III been
bɪn, biːn

To be has various meanings. It means to have existence or life and is also used to introduce a characteristic or condition of something. To be is also an auxiliary verb.

1 – 00:15 ☐ 4

become

I become
bɪˈkʌm

II became
bɪˈkeɪm

III become
bɪˈkʌm

To become means to begin to exist, or to change from one state of being or role to another.

1 – 01:06 ☐ 7

begin

I begin
bɪˈgɪn

II began / begun
bɪˈgæn / bɪˈgʌn

III begun
bɪˈgʌn

To begin means to initiate something.

1 – 01:50 ☐ 9

break

I break
breɪk

II broke
brəʊk

III broken
ˈbrəʊkən

To break means using some force (intentionally or accidentally) to split something into multiple pieces.

1 – 02:30 19

bring

I bring
brɪŋ

II brought
brɔːt

III brought
brɔːt

To bring means to cause something or someone to move with you from one place to another.

1 – 03:13 22

build

I build
bɪld

II built
bɪlt

III built
bɪlt

To build means to form or create something (usually out of other materials).

1 – 03:54 24

buy

I buy
baɪ

II bought
bɔːt

III bought
bɔːt

To buy means to give money to a person or business in exchange for goods or services.

1 – 04:34 ☐ 28

can

I can
kən / kæn

II could
kəd / kʊd

III been able to
biːn ˈeɪbl tə

Can is a modal verb that means having the quality of being able to do something.

1 – 05:16 ☐ 29

choose

I choose
tʃuːz

II chose
tʃəʊz

III chosen
ˈtʃəʊzn

To choose means to pick something (usually out of two or more options).

1 – 05:58 ☐ 33

come

I come
kʌm

II came
keɪm

III come
kʌm

To move or travel towards the location of the speaker. "Come" is very often the opposite, directionally, of "go".

1 – 06:39 35

cost

I cost
kɒst

II cost
kɒst

III cost
kɒst

To cost means the price of something that is for sale; the quantity of money needed to purchase something. We say something costs twelve euros.

1 – 07:23 36

cut

I cut
kʌt

II cut
kʌt

III cut
kʌt

To cut means to use some type of sharp object to pierce or slice through the surface of something.

1 – 08:10 39

do

I do
də, du

II did
dɪd

III done
dʌn

To do means to execute an action. To do is also an auxiliary verb.

1 – 08:51 43

draw

I draw
drɔː

II drew
druː

III drawn
drɔːn

To draw means to use a writing tool (like a pen, pencil, or marker) to put lines or shapes on a surface, often to create a picture.

1 – 09:32 44

drink

I drink
drɪŋk

II drank
dræŋk

III drunk / drank
drʌŋk / dræŋk

To drink means to ingest liquid through the mouth.

1 – 10:18 46

drive

I drive
draɪv

II drove
drəʊv

III driven
ˈdrɪvn

To drive means to use the controls of a vehicle, such as a car, boat, or train, to cause it to move in a specific direction.

1 – 10:59 47

eat

I eat
iːt

II ate
eɪt, et

III eaten
ˈiːtn

To eat means to put food into your mouth and to chew and swallow it.

1 – 11:45 49

fall

I fall
fɔːl

II fell
fel

III fallen
ˈfɔːlən

To fall means to drop towards the earth from either a small or great height when not supported by something.

1 – 12:25 50

feel

I feel
fiːl

II felt
felt

III felt
felt

To feel has more than one meaning, including to discern something using touch, and to have emotions or physical sensations.

1 – 13:08 52

find

I find
faɪnd

II found
faʊnd

III found
faʊnd

To find means to encounter something that you did not know the location of, or that you previously did not know existed.

1 – 13:53 54

fly

I fly
flaɪ

II flew
fluː

III flown
fləʊn

To fly means to travel through the air (above the ground). It also means riding in a plane while it travels through the air.

1 – 14:37 58

forget

I forget
fəˈget

II forgot
fəˈgɒt

III forgotten / forgot ★
fəˈgɒtn / fəˈgɒt ★

To forget means to stop remembering something.

1 – 15:21 64

get

I get
get

II got
gɒt

III got / gotten ★
gɒt / ˈgɒtn ★

To get means to acquire, gain, or be given something.

1 – 16:03 68

give

I give
gɪv

II gave
geɪv

III given
ˈgɪvn

To give means to provide something to someone without getting anything in exchange. It also means to hand something to another person.

1 – 16:44 71

go

I go
gəʊ

II went
went

III gone / been
gɒn / biːn

To go means to take yourself from one place to another.

1 – 17:28 72

grow

I grow
grəʊ

II grew
gruː

III grown
grəʊn

To grow means to expand in some way, such as size or number.

1 – 18:09 74

have

I have
həv, əv, hæv

II had
həd, əd, hæd

III had
həd, əd, hæd

To have has various meanings; owning or holding something. It also means doing some specific actions, such as having a conversation. To have is also an auxiliary verb.

1 – 18:49 77

hear

I hear
hɪə(r)

II heard
hɜːd

III heard
hɜːd

To hear means to discern sounds with the ears.

1 – 19:38 ☐ 78

keep

I keep
kiːp

II kept
kept

III kept
kept

To keep has various meanings; holding on to something belonging to you, and securing someone or something in a location so that they remain there.

1 – 20:16 ☐ 85

know

I know
nəʊ

II knew
njuː

III known
nəʊn

To know means to be familiar with a person or place or to have awareness or understanding of a topic, idea, or piece of information.

1 – 21:01 ☐ 88

learn

I learn
lɜːn

II learnt / learned
lɜːnt / lɜːnd

III learnt / learned
lɜːnt / lɜːnd

To learn means to attain comprehension of ideas, skills, or information.

1 – 21:46 ☐ 93

leave

I leave
liːv

II left
left

III left
left

To leave means to depart from somewhere.

1 – 22:33 ☐ 94

let

I let
let

II let
let

III let
let

To let means to permit an action to occur, or to allow someone to carry out an action.

1 – 23:11 ☐ 96

lie

I lie
laɪ

II lay
leɪ

III lain
leɪn

To lie means to be in, or put your body into, a reclining position on the ground or another surface so that you are horizontal.

1 – 23:53 97

lose

I lose
luːz

II lost
lɒst

III lost
lɒst

To lose means to be unable to find something because it was misplaced or is not where it should be or usually belongs.

1 – 24:37 99

make

I make
meɪk

II made
meɪd

III made
meɪd

To make has several meanings. These include producing, or building something, compelling someone to carry out an action, and to do something (used with specific actions).

1 – 25:21 100

mean

I mean
mi:n

II meant
ment

III meant
ment

To mean refers to the definition of something (usually a word or phrase), which is represented by that word or phrase. In this meaning, it is commonly used in the question, "What does that mean?" when we ask for a definition or explanation. To mean is also used to show a person's intent or the intended use of an object.

1 – 26:09 101

meet

I meet
mi:t

II met
met

III met
met

To meet has several meanings, including encountering and becoming familiar with someone for the first time, and converging in the same place with another person or other people.

1 – 27:09 102

mistake

I mistake
mɪˈsteɪk

II mistook
mɪˈstʊk

III mistaken
mɪˈsteɪkən

To mistake means to misinterpret or misunderstand something, and it also means to identify a person or object incorrectly.

1 – 27:56 105

pay

I pay
peɪ

II paid
peɪd

III paid
peɪd

To pay means to provide someone with money in exchange for something.

1 – 28:42 124

put

I put
pʊt

II put
pʊt

III put
pʊt

To put means to place an object (or sometimes a person) into a particular location or position.

1 – 29:21 127

read

I read
ri:d

II read
red

III read
red

To read means to look at and understand meaning from letters and words.

1 – 30:03 129

ride

I ride
raɪd

II rode
rəʊd

III ridden
ˈrɪdn

To ride means to be carried on the back of an animal or on or in a vehicle of some kind.

1 – 30:43 138

run

I run
rʌn

II ran
ræn

III run
rʌn

To run means to travel by foot at a very rapid pace that includes moments when neither foot is touching the ground.

1 – 31:25 141

say

I say
seɪ

II said
sed

III said
sed

To say means to use the voice to produce words.

1 – 32:09 143

see

I see
siː

II saw
sɔː

III seen
siːn

To see means to discern with the eyes.

1 – 32:48 144

sell

I sell
sel

II sold
səʊld

III sold
səʊld

To sell means to provide someone with something in exchange for money.

1 – 33:27 146

send

I send
send

II sent
sent

III sent
sent

To send means to cause or arrange for something to be transmitted from one place to another (such as a letter, package, email, or other digital messages).

1 – 34:07 147

show

I show
ʃəʊ

II showed
ʃəʊd

III shown / showed
ʃəʊn / ʃəʊd

To show means to put something before another person to be looked at or direct someone's attention to something for the same purpose.

1 – 34:54 154

sing

I sing
sɪŋ

II sang
sæŋ

III sung
sʌŋ

To sing means to create music with the voice.

1 – 35:40 157

sit

I sit
sɪt

II sat
sæt

III sat
sæt

To sit means to bend your legs in some way to rest your weight on your buttocks and the backs of your thighs while maintaining your back in a vertical position.

1 – 36:19 159

sleep

I sleep
sliːp

II slept
slept

III slept
slept

To sleep means to be in a relaxed and naturally occurring state of unconsciousness during which the body rejuvenates (in humans, this usually happens for several hours during the night).

1 – 37:05 161

speak

I speak
spiːk

II spoke
spəʊk

III spoken
ˈspəʊkən

To speak means to use the voice to produce words. It also means having the ability to converse in a language.

1 – 37:53 167

spell

I spell
spel

II spelt / spelled
spelt / speld

III spelt / spelled
spelt / speld

To spell means to put letters of an alphabet together to form a word.

1 – 38:37 168

spend

I spend
spend

II spent
spent

III spent
spent

To spend means to give out money to buy something. It also means to pass the time or expend energy.

1 – 39:23 169

stand

I stand
stænd

II stood
stʊd

III stood
stʊd

To stand means to balance the body vertically with the weight in the feet or to move from another position into this one.

1 – 40:07 177

swim

I swim
swɪm

II swam
swæm

III swum
swʌm

To swim means to use different parts of the body (which vary between people and various types of animals) to cause oneself to travel through water.

1 – 40:51 192

take

I take
teɪk

II took
tʊk

III taken
ˈteɪkən

To take has many meanings. One of the most common is to bring something into your possession or grip, and another is to carry out specific actions (such as take a walk, take a vacation, take a few steps).

1 – 41:37 194

teach

I teach
tiːtʃ

II taught
tɔːt

III taught
tɔːt

To teach means to educate or inform someone about a subject, information, or skill.

1 – 42:27 195

tell

I tell
tel

II told
təʊld

III told
təʊld

To tell means to speak to someone to give them information or recount a story.

1 – 43:09 197

think

I think
θɪŋk

II thought
θɔːt

III thought
θɔːt

To think means to have an opinion, or to have or process thoughts or ideas in your mind.

1 – 43:49 198

understand

I understand
ˌʌndəˈstænd

II understood
ˌʌndəˈstʊd

III understood
ˌʌndəˈstʊd

To understand means knowing or perceiving the intended meaning of something, such as words, language, or others' actions.

1 – 44:32 205

wake

I wake
weɪk

II woke / waked ★
wəʊk / weɪkt ★

III woken / waked ★
ˈwəʊkən / weɪkt ★

To wake means to return to consciousness from a state of sleep or interrupt another's sleep to bring them back into a conscious state.

1 – 45:17 212

wear

I wear
weə(r)

II wore
wɔː(r)

III worn
wɔːn

To wear something means to be clothed in that thing.

1 – 46:05 213

win

I win
wɪn

II won
wʌn

III won
wʌn

To win means to earn first place in some activity involving competition.

1 – 46:45 218

write

I write
raɪt

II wrote
rəʊt

III written
ˈrɪtn

To write has a variety of related meanings, including to use a pen, pencil, computer, or other physical or digital methods to record words or characters from an alphabet on a surface or in a digital document. It also means to use written language to record or create a story or other content designed to be read.

1 – 47:25 ☐ 224

LEVEL

A2

beat

I beat
biːt

II beat
biːt

III beaten / beat ★
ˈbiːtn / biːt ★

To beat means to strike a blow to a person or object again and again.

2 – 00:15 6

blow

I blow
bləʊ

II blew
bluː

III blown
bləʊn

To blow means to cause air to move. This can be an occurrence of nature, like wind, or a human action where one pushes air out of the lungs through the mouth.

2 – 00:59 18

burn

I burn
bɜːn

II burnt / burned
bɜːnt / bɜːnd

III burnt / burned
bɜːnt / bɜːnd

To burn means to be damaged by or to damage something with fire. This may refer to superficial damage or destruction.

2 – 01:45 25

catch

I catch
kætʃ

II caught
kɔːt

III caught
kɔːt

To catch has several meanings, including to use the hands (or something else) to receive an object that was thrown, to use the hands (or something else) to cause a moving object to stop and remain still, and to prevent someone or something from getting away.

2 – 02:35 31

deal

I deal
diːl

II dealt
delt

III dealt
delt

To deal means to give something out to different people (commonly used to refer to the action of passing out the cards in a game).

2 – 03:28 40

dream

I dream
dri:m

II dreamt / dreamed
dremt / dri:md

III dreamt / dreamed
dremt / dri:md

To dream means to see or experience things in your mind while you are sleeping, often in the form of images that you sometimes remember when you wake up.

2 – 04:11 45

feed

I feed
fi:d

II fed
fed

III fed
fed

To feed means to provide food to someone (a person or animal).

2 – 05:02 51

fight

I fight
faɪt

II fought
fɔ:t

III fought
fɔ:t

To fight means to work against someone (or something) in an attempt to do damage to or destroy them. This can occur between individuals or on a larger scale, such as a battle or war.

2 – 05:42 53

fit

I fit
fɪt

II fitted / fit ★
ˈfɪtɪd / fɪt ★

III fitted / fit ★
ˈfɪtɪd / fɪt ★

To fit has several meanings, including to have the proper dimensions and shape required (such as a jigsaw piece in a puzzle), and to evaluate the size and shape of a person to create custom items for them (such as shoes or clothes).

2 – 06:32 ☐ 55

hide

I hide
haɪd

II hid
hɪd

III hidden
ˈhɪdn

To hide means to move yourself or another person or thing into a place or position where it won't be seen or found.

2 – 07:28 ☐ 79

hit

I hit
hɪt

II hit
hɪt

III hit
hɪt

To hit means to use an object or part of your body to strike someone or something, often violently.

2 – 08:11 ☐ 80

hold

I hold
həʊld

II held
held

III held
held

To hold means to have something in your hand or to keep something within another thing (for example, the glass holds water).

2 – 08:53 ☐ 81

hurt

I hurt
hɜːt

II hurt
hɜːt

III hurt
hɜːt

To hurt means to inflict damage (emotional or physical) on a person or animal, or to feel the same.

2 – 09:36 ☐ 82

lead

I lead
liːd

II led
led

III led
led

To lead means to conduct someone from one place to another, usually with you in front and the other person following. This can be a physical journey, but we can also lead someone to an idea. To lead also means to be in charge (for example, in charge of a company, country, military unit, and so forth).

2 – 10:19 ☐ 90

lend

I lend
lend

II lent
lent

III lent
lent

To lend means to give money or an object to someone to use for some time before returning it. In the case of money, they would return an amount based on the agreed-upon terms.

2 – 11:16 95

light

I light
laɪt

II lit / lighted ★
lɪt / ˈlaɪtɪd ★

III lit / lighted ★
lɪt / ˈlaɪtɪd ★

To light means to cause something to catch fire.

2 – 12:03 98

ring

I ring
rɪŋ

II rang
ræŋ

III rung
rʌŋ

To ring means to call someone on the phone (mainly in British English). It also means to move a bell to make it give off a sound.

2 – 12:47 139

rise

I rise
raɪz

II rose
rəʊz

III risen
ˈrɪzn

To rise means to move from a lower to a higher position.

2 – 13:31 140

shake

I shake
ʃeɪk

II shook
ʃʊk

III shaken
ˈʃeɪkən

To shake means to move rapidly back and forth in small movements, often like vibration, or to move something else rapidly back and forth in small or large movements.

2 – 14:10 150

shut

I shut
ʃʌt

II shut
ʃʌt

III shut
ʃʌt

To shut means to move something from an open into a closed position, for example, a lid, door, curtain, or box can be shut.

2 – 14:58 156

smell

I smell
smel

II smelt / smelled
smelt / smeld

III smelt / smelled
smelt / smeld

To smell means to discern scents with the nose. It also means to give off a scent.

2 – 15:44 164

steal

I steal
stiːl

II stole
stəʊl

III stolen
ˈstəʊlən

To steal means to take possession of something that does not belong to you and to do so without the permission of the rightful owner.

2 – 16:31 178

throw

I throw
θrəʊ

II threw
θruː

III thrown
θrəʊn

To throw means to use your hand to launch something through the air and away from you.

2 – 17:16 200

wet

I wet
wet

II wet / wetted
wet / ˈwetɪd

III wet / wetted
wet / ˈwetɪd

To wet means to cause something to become damp or drenched with liquid of some kind.

2 – 17:57 217

LEVEL

B1

awake

I awake
əˈweɪk

II awoke / awaked ★
əˈwəʊk / əˈweɪkt ★

III awoken / awaked ★ / awoke ★
əˈwəʊkən / əˈweɪkt ★ / əˈwəʊk ★

To awake means to return to a state of being awake or conscious, usually from a state of sleep.

3 – 00:15 ☐ 2

babysit

I babysit / baby-sit ★
ˈbeɪbisɪt / ˈbeɪbisɪt ★

II babysat / babysate / baby-sat ★
ˈbeɪbisæt / ˈbeɪbi seɪt / ˈbeɪbisæt ★

III babysat / babysitten / baby-sat ★
ˈbeɪbisæt / ˈbeɪbisætən / ˈbeɪbisæt ★

To babysit means to take care of a child (usually not your own) for a relatively short period.

3 – 01:05 ☐ 3

bend

I bend
bend

II bent
bent

III bent
bent

To bend means to cause something to become curved (usually by applying some degree of force).

3 – 02:03 ☐ 10

bite

I bite
baɪt

II bit
bɪt

III bitten
ˈbɪtn

To bite means to grip something with your teeth and often to use the teeth to do damage.

3 – 02:45 16

breastfeed

I breastfeed
ˈbrestfiːd

II breastfed
ˈbrestfed

III breastfed
ˈbrestfed

To breastfeed means to nourish a baby with the milk from a mother's breast.

3 – 03:25 20

freeze

I freeze
friːz

II froze
frəʊz

III frozen
ˈfrəʊzn

To freeze means to change something from a liquid to a solid by exposing it to very cold temperatures.

3 – 04:07 67

hang

I hang
hæŋ

II hung / hanged
hʌŋ / hæŋd

III hung / hanged
hʌŋ / hæŋd

To hang has more than one meaning, including connecting something to support from above so that it doesn't touch the ground.

3 – 04:50 ☐ 76

knit

I knit
nɪt

II knit / knitted
nɪt / ˈnɪtɪd

III knit / knitted
nɪt / ˈnɪtɪd

To knit means to use two (or more) long, straight needles to intertwine yarn in different patterns to make clothes or other things.

3 – 05:38 ☐ 87

lay

I lay
leɪ

II laid
leɪd

III laid
leɪd

To lay means to place something onto a surface, often in a horizontal orientation.

3 – 06:27 ☐ 89

prove

I prove
pruːv

II proved
pruːvd

III proved /proven ★
pruːvd / ˈpruːvn, ˈprəʊvn ★

To prove means to present some type of evidence to illustrate that something is true.

3 – 07:08 126

quit

I quit
kwɪt

II quit / quitted
kwɪt / ˈkwɪtɪd

III quit / quitted
kwɪt / ˈkwɪtɪd

To quit means to cease an action, or to leave a job permanently.

3 – 07:52 128

set

I set
set

II set
set

III set
set

To set has more than one meaning, including to put something in a particular place, and to secure something into a position.

3 – 08:36 148

sew

I sew
səʊ

II sewed
səʊd

III sewn / sewed
səʊn / səʊd

To sew means to stitch things together with thread or another type of long, thin, flexible material.

3 – 09:20 ☐ 149

shine

I shine
ʃaɪn

II shone
ʃɒn

III shone
ʃɒn

To shine means to radiate light or to be bright because of reflected light.

3 – 10:05 ☐ 152

shoot

I shoot
ʃu:t

II shot
ʃɒt

III shot
ʃɒt

To shoot means to cause something to be projected forward suddenly and rapidly from some type of weapon, such as a bullet from a gun or an arrow from a bow. It also means to hit someone with the projectile from a weapon (usually resulting in injury or death).

3 – 10:47 ☐ 153

sink

I sink
sɪŋk

II sank
sæŋk

III sunk
sʌŋk

To sink means to move from a higher to a lower position, often within water or another liquid. It also means to cause something to enter a body of liquid and move downward toward the bottom.

3 – 11:40 158

spread

I spread
spred

II spread
spred

III spread
spred

To spread means to disperse something over a surface or area.

3 – 12:28 175

stick

I stick
stɪk

II stuck
stʌk

III stuck
stʌk

To stick has multiple meanings, causing something to bond to something else by using materials such as glue or a type of fastener or pin and pushing something sharp or pointing into someone or something.

3 – 13:09 179

string

I string
strɪŋ

II strung
strʌŋ

III strung
strʌŋ

To string means to join items together using a string, thread, or cord (like beads on a string).

🔈 3 – 13:58 ☐ 185

swell

I swell
swell

II swelled
sweld

III swollen / swelled ★
ˈswəʊlən / sweld ★

To swell means to expand, often due to an increased amount of liquid or gas from the inside.

🔈 3 – 14:42 ☐ 191

upset

I upset
ʌpˈset

II upset
ʌpˈset

III upset
ʌpˈset

To upset means to cause someone to become distressed in some way.

🔈 3 – 15:27 ☐ 211

LEVEL

B2

arise

I arise
əˈraɪz

II arose
əˈrəʊz

III arisen
əˈrɪzn

To arise has more than one meaning. It is used to say something stems from a specific place, idea, or source. It also means moving from a sitting or lying position to a standing position. And it means to begin to exist.

4 – 00:15 ☐ 1

bear

I bear
beə(r)

II bore
bɔː(r)

III born / borne
bɔːn / bɔːn

To bear can mean to hold something and move it from one place to another (physically, or a message), to endure something (usually something negative), or to give birth to a child.

4 – 01:07 ☐ 5

bet

I bet
bet

II bet / betted ★
bet / ˈbɛtɪd ★

III bet / betted ★
bet / ˈbɛtɪd ★

To bet means to put money on the line against the outcome of something in the future (often some type of competition), and a person will win or lose the bet based on whether they were correct in guessing the outcome.

4 – 01:58 ☐ 12

bid

I bid
bɪd

II bid / bade ★
bɪd / beɪd, bæd ★

III bid / bade ★ / bidden ★
bɪd / beɪd, bæd ★ / ˈbɪdn ★

To bid means to put forward an amount of money or services you are willing to provide in exchange for something.

4 – 02:52 ☐ 14

broadcast

I broadcast
ˈbrɔːdkɑːst

II broadcast / broadcasted
ˈbrɔːdkɑːst / ˈbrɔːdkɑːstɪd

III broadcast / broadcasted
ˈbrɔːdkɑːst / ˈbrɔːdkɑːstɪd

To broadcast means to cause radio or television signals to be broadly emitted so that they can be received and consumed by others.

4 – 03:40 ☐ 23

cast

I cast
kɑːst

II cast
kɑːst

III cast
kɑːst

To cast means to use force to propel something (often away from oneself).

4 – 04:33 ☐ 30

dig

I dig
dɪg

II dug
dʌg

III dug
dʌg

To dig means to use a tool or part of the body to remove earth from an area to create a hole.

4 – 05:14 ☐ 41

dive

I dive
daɪv

II dived / dove
daɪvd / dəʊv

III dived
daɪvd

To dive means to enter a body of water headfirst. It also means to drop rapidly.

4 – 05:55 ☐ 42

forbid

I forbid
fəˈbɪd

II forbade / forbad
fəˈbæd, fəˈbeɪd / fəˈbæd

III forbidden
fəˈbɪdn

To forbid means to state that something is explicitly not allowed.

4 – 06:41 ☐ 60

forecast

I forecast
ˈfɔːkɑːst

II forecast / forecasted
ˈfɔːkɑːst / ˈfɔːkɑːstɪd

III forecast / forecasted
ˈfɔːkɑːst / ˈfɔːkɑːstɪd

To forecast means to put forth expected details about the future, usually logical deductions based on the present information.

4 – 07:25 ☐ 61

forgive

I forgive
fəˈgɪv

II forgave
fəˈgeɪv

III forgiven
fəˈgɪvn

To forgive means to release anger and blame felt toward a person who has done something against you.

4 – 08:18 ☐ 65

input

I input
ˈɪnpʊt

II input / inputted
ˈɪnpʊt / ˈɪnpʊtɪd

III input / inputted
ˈɪnpʊt / ˈɪnpʊtɪd

To input means to record data into some type of program (usually on a computer).

4 – 09:00 ☐ 83

kneel

I kneel
niːl

II knelt / kneeled
nelt / niːld

III knelt / kneeled
nelt / niːld

To kneel means to be in (or move into) a position with your knees touching the ground and supporting your weight.

4 – 09:47 ☐ 86

lean

I lean
liːn

II leant / leaned
lent / liːnd

III leant / leaned
lent / liːnd

To lean means to put something against something else for support so that the first object is at a slope. A person can also lean against something, and both people and things can lean in a direction (in a bent or sloped position) without support.

4 – 10:35 ☐ 91

misunderstand

I misunderstand
ˌmɪsʌndəˈstænd

II misunderstood
ˌmɪsʌndəˈstʊd

III misunderstood
ˌmɪsʌndəˈstʊd

To misunderstand means to understand something incorrectly.

4 – 11:33 106

output

I output
ˈaʊtpʊt

II output / outputted
ˈaʊtpʊt / ˈaʊtpʊtɪd

III output / outputted
ˈaʊtpʊt / ˈaʊtpʊtɪd

To output means to provide or create something.

4 – 12:16 110

overcome

I overcome
ˌəʊvəˈkʌm

II overcame
ˌəʊvəˈkeɪm

III overcome
ˌəʊvəˈkʌm

To overcome means to conquer something (such as a challenge) successfully, and it also means to be made powerless or weak as a result of strong emotion or some physical state.

4 – 13:02 113

oversleep

I oversleep
ˌəʊvəˈsliːp

II overslept
ˌəʊvəˈslept

III overslept
ˌəʊvəˈslept

To oversleep means to sleep longer than when you intended to wake up, often past the time of an alarm.

4 – 13:52 ☐ 119

overtake

I overtake
ˌəʊvəˈteɪk

II overtook
ˌəʊvəˈtʊk

III overtaken
ˌəʊvəˈteɪkən

To overtake means to come from behind another person, vehicle, or other moving thing and to draw level with or pass them. It can also be used for people working on tasks.

4 – 14:37 ☐ 120

overwrite

I overwrite
ˌəʊvəˈraɪt

II overwrote
ˌəʊvəˈrəʊt

III overwritten
ˌəʊvəˈrɪtn

To overwrite means to save data (for example, in a computer) in the same location as other existing data in a way that causes the original data to be erased.

4 – 15:26 ☐ 122

rebuild

I rebuild
ˌriːˈbɪld

II rebuilt
ˌriːˈbɪlt

III rebuilt
ˌriːˈbɪlt

To rebuild means constructing something for a second time (often after the first version has been partially or fully destroyed).

4 – 16:15 130

repay

I repay
rɪˈpeɪ

II repaid
rɪˈpeɪd

III repaid
rɪˈpeɪd

To repay means to give money to someone equal to an amount that was previously borrowed from them.

4 – 17:00 132

retake

I retake
ˌriːˈteɪk

II retook
ˌriːˈtʊk

III retaken
ˌriːˈteɪkən

To retake means to take something for a second time (or third, or fourth, and so on). Particularly something you previously possessed (for an object) or that you had already taken (for a test or exam).

4 – 17:42 133

retell

I retell
ˌriːˈtel

II retold
ˌriːˈtəʊld

III retold
ˌriːˈtəʊld

To retell means to repeat a story or piece of information again or in another way.

4 – 18:34 134

rewrite

I rewrite
ˌriːˈraɪt

II rewrote
ˌriːˈrəʊt

III rewritten
ˌriːˈrɪtn

To rewrite means to go through the writing process again for something that was previously written, usually while making changes to improve the new finished product.

4 – 19:18 137

seek

I seek
siːk

II sought
sɔːt

III sought
sɔːt

To seek means to attempt to discover or encounter something, or to search for something.

4 – 20:05 145

slide

I slide
slaɪd

II slid
slɪd

III slid / slidden
slɪd / slɪdn

To slide means moving across a smooth surface, often quickly and usually through momentum (for example, if a person or animal slides, it means they are not taking individual steps).

4 – 20:47 ☐ 162

spill

I spill
spɪl

II spilt / spilled
spɪlt / spɪld

III spilt / spilled
spɪlt / spɪld

To spill means to let something (often a liquid) fall out of its container either accidentally or on purpose.

4 – 21:39 ☐ 170

split

I split
splɪt

II split
splɪt

III split
splɪt

To split means to cleave something into two or more pieces or to be broken apart by something.

4 – 22:28 ☐ 173

spoil

I spoil
spɔɪl

II spoilt / spoiled
spɔɪlt / spɔɪld

III spoilt / spoiled
spɔɪlt / spɔɪld

To spoil means to cause or permit something to decay or break down.

4 – 23:11 174

spring

I spring
sprɪŋ

II sprang / sprung ★
spræŋ / sprʌŋ ★

III sprung
sprʌŋ

To spring means to jump or leap upward, over or across something, or into action.

4 – 23:57 176

strike

I strike
strike

II struck
strʌk

III struck / stricken
strʌk / ˈstrɪkən

To strike has various meanings; using an object or part of the body to hit someone or something, and members of a workforce stopping work for some time to pressure an employer to make changes to working conditions.

4 – 24:43 184

swear

I swear
sweə(r)

II swore
swɔː(r)

III sworn
swɔːn

To swear means to make a pledge or vow. It also means to speak words that are generally considered to be vulgar or otherwise offensive.

4 – 25:37 ☐ 188

sweat

I sweat
swet

II sweat / sweated
swet / ˈswetɪd

III sweat / sweated
swet / ˈswetɪd

To sweat means to exude moisture from the skin because of excessive heat or physical exertion.

4 – 26:23 ☐ 189

sweep

I sweep
swiːp

II swept / sweeped
swept / swiːpt

III swept / sweeped
swept / swiːpt

To sweep means move a broom, brush, or other objects across a surface repeatedly to clean it.

4 – 27:10 ☐ 190

tear

I tear
teə(r)

II tore
tɔː(r)

III torn
tɔːn

To tear means to rip pieces off something or create a hole in something by the same means (often roughly or violently, and commonly used with materials such as paper or cloth).

4 – 27:58 ☐ 196

thrust

I thrust
θrʌst

II thrust
θrʌst

III thrust
θrʌst

To thrust means to apply force to propel something forcefully in a direction.

4 – 28:47 ☐ 201

undergo

I undergo
ˌʌndəˈgəʊ

II underwent
ˌʌndəˈwent

III undergone
ˌʌndəˈgɒn

To undergo means to experience something difficult or painful to some degree (this could be physical, mental, or emotional pain).

4 – 29:29 ☐ 203

undertake

I undertake
ˌʌndəˈteɪk

II undertook
ˌʌndəˈtʊk

III undertaken
ˌʌndəˈteɪkən

To undertake means to begin to carry out an action or task, or to agree to do so.

4 – 30:15 ☐ 206

undo

I undo
ʌnˈduː

II undid
ʌnˈdɪd

III undone
ʌnˈdʌn

To undo has more than one meaning, including to release a fastening (such as a button on a shirt), or to damage a person's prominence, standing, or position in society.

4 – 30:59 ☐ 208

wind (1)

I wind
wɪnd

II winded
ˈwɪndɪd

III winded
ˈwɪndɪd

To wind means to cause someone to lose their breath for a while (it is often used in the passive voice).

4 – 31:47 ☐ 219

wind (2)

I wind
waɪnd

II wound
waʊnd

III wound
waʊnd

To wind means to wrap one thing around something else or rotate a part of something mechanical to operate it or cause it to continue working on its own.

4 – 32:30 220

withdraw

I withdraw
wɪðˈdrɔː, wɪθˈdrɔː

II withdrew
wɪðˈdruː, wɪθˈdruː

III withdrawn
wɪðˈdrɔːn, wɪθˈdrɔːn

To withdraw means to take something away from or out of a place (frequently money out of a bank account) or to leave a location.

4 – 33:16 221

LEVEL

C1

befall

I befall
bɪˈfɔːl

II befell
bɪˈfel

III befallen
bɪˈfɔːlən

To befall means to occur, either independently or to a person or thing.

5 – 00:15 ☐ 8

bequeath

I bequeath
bɪˈkwiːð

II bequeathed / bequethed / bequoth / bequod
bɪˈkwiːðd / biːkwɛtɛd / biːkwəʊθ / biːkwɒd

III bequeathed / bequethed / bequoth / bequethen
bɪˈkwiːðd / biːkwɛtɛd / biːkwəʊθ / biːkwɛtɛn

To bequeath means to specify (often in a formal document) that something (usually a possession) will belong to another person when you die.

5 – 00:58 ☐ 11

bind

I bind
baɪnd

II bound
baʊnd

III bound
baʊnd

To bind means to use rope, string, cord (or something similar) to tie items together or hold them in place.

5 – 01:59 ☐ 15

bleed

I bleed
bli:d

II bled
bled

III bled
bled

To bleed means having blood come out of the body (often through some type of wound).

5 – 02:43 17

breed

I breed
bri:d

II bred
bred

III bred
bred

To breed means to plan and control the reproduction of animals or plants to achieve a specific result in their offspring.

5 – 03:24 21

burst

I burst
bɜ:st

II burst / bursted ★
bɜ:st / ˈbɜ:stɪd ★

III burst / bursted ★
bɜ:st / ˈbɜ:stɪd ★

To burst means to rupture or split due to excessive tension or pressure from the inside of something.

5 – 04:07 26

bust

I bust
bʌst

II bust / busted ★
bʌst / ˈbʌstɪd ★

III bust / busted ★
bʌst / ˈbʌstɪd ★

To bust means to split, fracture, damage, or in some other way to break something.

5 – 04:54 ☐ 27

cling

I cling
klɪŋ

II clung
klʌŋ

III clung
klʌŋ

To cling means to grip something tightly, often with resistance to letting go.

5 – 05:40 ☐ 34

creep

I creep
kriːp

II crept
krept

III crept
krept

To creep means to travel across the ground with the body in a low position near the ground.

5 – 06:22 ☐ 38

dwell

I dwell
dwel

II dwelt / dwelled ★
dwelt / dweld ★

III dwelt / dwelled ★
dwelt / dweld ★

To dwell means to occupy a place permanently or semi-permanently, as in the place where you live.

5 – 07:03 48

flee

I flee
fliː

II fled
fled

III fled
fled

To flee means to move away from a thing, person, or place at a rapid speed to escape (often because of real or perceived danger).

5 – 07:49 56

fling

I fling
flɪŋ

II flung
flʌŋ

III flung
flʌŋ

To fling means to propel something away from you abruptly.

5 – 08:34 57

foresee

I foresee
fɔːˈsiː

II foresaw
fɔːˈsɔː

III foreseen
fɔːˈsiːn

To foresee means to identify or view something in the future before it happens.

5 – 09:14 ☐ 62

grind

I grind
graɪnd

II ground
graʊnd

III ground
graʊnd

To grind means to change something from a larger solid piece (or pieces) into tiny pieces or powder by some type of crushing, usually with the aid of a tool.

5 – 09:57 ☐ 73

handwrite

I handwrite
hændraɪt

II handwrote
hændrəʊt

III handwritten
hændˈrɪt(ə)n

To handwrite means to use the hands and a writing implement (such as a pen, pencil, marker, etc.) to write on something.

5 – 10:44 ☐ 75

leap

I leap
liːp

II leapt / leaped
lept / liːpt

III leapt / leaped
lept / liːpt

To leap means propelling yourself off the ground, often over an object or space (used for both humans and animals).

5 – 11:30 92

mislead

I mislead
ˌmɪsˈliːd

II misled
ˌmɪsˈled

III misled
ˌmɪsˈled

To mislead means to guide someone off the correct path (usually metaphorical rather than an actual physical path) into incorrect actions or behaviour. It also means to cause someone to believe something that isn't true.

5 – 12:18 103

overdo

I overdo
ˌəʊvəˈduː

II overdid
ˌəʊvəˈdɪd

III overdone
ˌəʊvəˈdʌn

To overdo means to do something more than is necessary or advisable. It is also used to say that something has been cooked past the point of being done.

5 – 13:10 114

overdraw

I overdraw
ˌəʊvəˈdrɔː

II overdrew
ˌəʊvəˈdruː

III overdrawn
ˌəʊvəˈdrɔːn

To overdraw means to spend or remove more money than exists in an account (resulting in a balance below zero).

5 - 13:57 ☐ 115

oversee

I oversee
ˌəʊvəˈsiː

II oversaw
ˌəʊvəˈsɔː

III overseen
ˌəʊvəˈsiːn

To oversee means paying close attention to another person's work to ensure that it is carried out and that it is carried out effectively.

5 - 14:43 ☐ 118

plead

I plead
pliːd

II pleaded / pled ★
ˈpliːdɪd / pled ★

III pleaded / pled ★
ˈpliːdɪd / pled ★

To plead has several meanings, including to make a formal statement of innocence or guilt in a court of law, and to implore someone for something.

5 - 15:29 ☐ 125

rethink

I rethink
ˌriːˈθɪŋk

II rethought
ˌriːˈθɔːt

III rethought
ˌriːˈθɔːt

To rethink means to contemplate something again, often with the possibility of changing your mind or opinion.

5 – 16:19 135

rewind

I rewind
ˌriːˈwaɪnd

II rewound
ˌriːˈwaʊnd

III rewound
ˌriːˈwaʊnd

To rewind means to wind something once more. It is commonly used to talk about music cassettes, VHS tapes, or film reels where winding them back resets them to the beginning.

5 – 17:03 136

shed

I shed
ʃed

II shed
ʃed

III shed
ʃed

To shed means to have something come off of something else, often a part that was previously attached to or part of the whole, such as the skin of a snake or butterfly shedding itself of its cocoon.

5 – 17:53 151

shrink

I shrink
ʃrɪŋk

II shrank / shrunk ★
ʃræŋk / ʃrʌŋk ★

III shrunk
ʃrʌŋk

To shrink means to reduce in size or to cause something else to reduce in size.

5 – 18:42 ☐ 155

sow

I sow
səʊ

II sowed
səʊd

III sown / sowed
səʊn / səʊd

To sow means to distribute seeds in the earth (either in an orderly or more haphazard fashion) to grow plants.

5 – 19:26 ☐ 166

spin

I spin
spɪn

II span / spun
spæn / spʌn

III spun
spʌn

To spin means to rotate in place (often quickly and repeatedly) or to cause something or someone else to do the same.

5 – 20:14 ☐ 171

stink

I stink
stɪŋk

II stank / stunk
stæŋk / stʌŋk

III stunk
stʌŋk

To stink means to have a very unpleasant odour.

5 – 21:01 181

strew

I strew
struː

II strewed
struːd

III strewn / strewed
struːn / struːd

To strew means to disperse something around an area or on a surface randomly.

5 – 21:43 182

stride

I stride
straɪd

II strode / strided
strəʊd / ˈstraɪdɪd

III stridden
ˈstrɪdn

To stride means to take long steps while walking. This word is often used to convey that someone is walking with confidence.

5 – 22:28 183

strive

I strive
straɪv

II strove / strived ★
strəʊv / straɪvd ★

III striven / strived ★
ˈstrɪvn / straɪvd ★

To strive means to work with effort and determination toward doing or achieving something.

5 – 23:17 186

swing

I swing
swɪŋ

II swung
swʌŋ

III swung
swʌŋ

To swing means to shift from one side to another while suspended, usually in an arcing motion.

5 – 24:06 193

thrive

I thrive
θraɪv

II throve / thrived
θrəʊv / θraɪvd

III thriven / thrived
ˈθrɪvn / θraɪvd

To thrive means to be extraordinarily successful in an activity or situation, due to or despite the circumstances.

5 – 24:49 199

underpay

I underpay
ˌʌndəˈpeɪ

II underpaid
ˌʌndəˈpeɪd

III underpaid
ˌʌndəˈpeɪd

To underpay means to pay an amount that is lower than merited or the agreed-upon price or amount.

5 – 25:39 204

unwind

I unwind
ˌʌnˈwaɪnd

II unwound
ˌʌnˈwaʊnd

III unwound
ˌʌnˈwaʊnd

To unwind means to undo something that is wound, coiled, or wrapped around something. It also means to ease tension or stress, especially in a person.

5 – 26:24 209

uphold

I uphold
ʌpˈhəʊld

II upheld
ʌpˈheld

III upheld
ʌpˈheld

To uphold means to sustain or nourish an idea, policy, or decision.

5 – 27:12 210

weave

I weave
wiːv

II wove
wəʊv

III woven
ˈwəʊvn

To weave means to create fabric or other material through interlacing threads, yarn, or fibres of some kind.

5 – 27:54 214

wed

I wed
wed

II wed / wedded
wed / ˈwedɪd

III wed / wedded
wed / ˈwedɪd

To wed means to get married (formally) to another person, or to perform a ceremony to unite people in marriage.

5 – 28:38 215

writhe

I writhe
raɪð

II wrothe / writhed
weɪkt / raɪðd

III writhen / writhed
rɪthɛn / raɪðd

To writhe means to squirm or to contort the position of something (for example, all or part of the body), often due to an intense physical sensation, such as pain or extreme discomfort.

5 – 29:26 225

LEVEL

C2

betake

I betake
bɪˈteɪk

II betook
bɪˈtʊk

III betaken
bɪˈteɪkən

To betake means to move yourself to a different place.

6 – 00:15 13

chide

I chide
tʃaɪd

II chid / chidden ★
tʃɪd / ˈtʃɪdn ★

III chid / chidden ★
tʃɪd / ˈtʃɪdn ★

To chide means to scold someone for something you disapprove of.

6 – 00:56 32

cowrite

I cowrite
kəʊraɪt

II cowrote
kəʊrəʊt

III cowritten
kəʊˈrɪtn

To cowrite means to collaborate with another person on the process of writing.

6 – 01:40 37

forbear

I forbear
fɔːˈbeə(r)

II forbore
fɔːˈbɔː(r)

III forborne / forborn
fɔːˈbɔːn / fɔːbɔːn

To forbear means to avoid doing or saying something, or to choose not to do or say it.

6 – 02:22 59

foretell

I foretell
fɔːˈtel

II foretold
fɔːˈtəʊld

III foretold
fɔːˈtəʊld

Like, foresee: To foretell means to identify or view something in the future before it happens.

6 – 03:10 63

forsake

I forsake
fəˈseɪk

II forsook
fəˈsʊk

III forsaken
fəˈseɪkən

To forsake has more than one meaning: it means to cease doing an action or habit that was formerly very important or to desert someone or something.

6 – 03:56 66

ghostwrite

I ghostwrite
gəʊstraɪt

II ghostwrote
gəʊstrəʊt

III ghostwritten
gəʊst ˈrɪtn

To ghostwrite means to write something for a different person who will then take credit for the work.

6 – 04:44 69

gird

I gird
gɜːd

II girded / girt
ˈgɜːdɪd / gɜːt

III girded / girt
ˈgɜːdɪd / gɜːt

To gird means to bind or encompass something with a flexible strap of some kind to secure it.

6 – 05:28 70

interweave

I interweave
ˌɪntəˈwiːv

II interwove
ˌɪntəˈwəʊv

III interwoven
ˌɪntəˈwəʊvn

To interweave means to entwine things together, connected to the idea of weaving fibres to make fabric.

6 – 06:16 84

misspend

I misspend
ˌmɪsˈspend

II misspent
ˌmɪsˈspent

III misspent
ˌmɪsˈspent

To misspend means to use money or time in a wasteful way.

6 – 07:01 ☐ 104

miswrite

I miswrite
mɪsraɪt

II miswrote
mɪsrəʊt

III miswritten
mɪsˈrɪtn

To miswrite means to write with errors.

6 – 07:44 ☐ 107

offset

I offset
ˈɒfset

II offset
ˈɒfset

III offset
ˈɒfset

To offset means to serve as an equal weight to balance something else (either physically or in the case of money or ideas).

6 – 08:25 ☐ 108

outlay

I outlay
ˈaʊtleɪ

II outlaid
aʊtˈleɪd

III outlaid
aʊtˈleɪd

To outlay means to disperse or expend money. The term is often used when the purpose of the expense is the beginning of a project (frequently in business).

6 – 09:11 109

outspend

I outspend
ˌaʊtˈspend

II outspent
ˌaʊtˈspent

III outspent
ˌaʊtˈspent

To outspend means to use more money than a specific limit (such as your income), or more than another person.

6 – 09:58 111

outwear

I outwear
aʊtˈweə

II outwore
aʊtˈwɔː

III outworn
aʊtˈwɔːn

To outwear (used to refer to items, clothing, or a particular type of material) means remaining in good condition longer than other similar things.

6 – 10:43 112

overeat

I overeat
ˌəʊvərˈiːt

II overate
ˌəʊvərˈet, ˌəʊvərˈeɪt

III overeaten
ˌəʊvərˈiːtn

To overeat means to eat more food than you need or is comfortable.

6 – 11:31 116

overhear

I overhear
ˌəʊvəˈhɪə(r)

II overheard
ˌəʊvəˈhɜːd

III overheard
ˌəʊvəˈhɜːd

To overhear means to hear something (intentionally or unintentionally) that was said to someone else. Often you overhear something without the speaker being aware that you have heard it.

6 – 12:14 117

overthrow

I overthrow
ˌəʊvəˈθrəʊ

II overthrew
ˌəʊvəˈθruː

III overthrown
ˌəʊvəˈθrəʊn

To overthrow means to remove a leader or government from power against their will.

6 – 13:04 121

partake

I partake
pɑːˈteɪk

II partook
pɑːˈtʊk

III partaken
pɑːˈteɪkən

To partake means participating in something with others (usually followed by the 'in' preposition), or consuming food or drink with others.

6 – 13:48 ☐ 123

rend

I rend
rend

II rent / rended
rent / ˈrɛndɪd

III rent / rended
rent / ˈrɛndɪd

To rend means to split something into pieces or off of something else, usually roughly or violently.

6 – 14:35 ☐ 131

saw

I saw
sɔː

II sawed
sɔːd

III sawn / sawed
sɔːn / sɔːd

To saw means using a tool, frequently a saw, to cut through something or to cut pieces off something with a back and forth motion.

6 – 15:23 ☐ 142

slay

I slay
sleɪ

II slew
sluː

III slain
sleɪn

To slay means to kill a person or animal, possibly in a violent manner, or (in the case of an animal) for food or sacrifice.

6 – 16:13 ☐ 160

sling

I sling
slɪŋ

II slung
slʌŋ

III slung
slʌŋ

To sling means to fling something into a different position (often abruptly and with force).

6 – 16:59 ☐ 163

sneak

I sneak
sniːk

II sneaked / snuck
sniːkt / snʌk

III sneaked / snuck
sniːkt / snʌk

To sneak means to move or go somewhere in a manner that is secretive and intended to avoid observation.

6 – 17:43 ☐ 165

spit

I spit
spɪt

II spat / spit ★
spæt / spɪt ★

III spat / spit ★
spæt / spɪt ★

To spit means to propel something out of the mouth (such as saliva or something else).

6 – 18:32 172

sting

I sting
stɪŋ

II stung
stʌŋ

III stung
stʌŋ

To sting means experiencing a sharp or burning pain (sometimes of the type caused by insects or plants that are mildly or extremely poisonous).

6 – 19:20 180

sublet

I sublet
ˌsʌbˈlet

II sublet
ˌsʌbˈlet

III sublet
ˌsʌbˈlet

To sublet means to rent to another person, all or part of something (usually a building or room) that you are paying rent for or renting something from someone under those circumstances.

6 – 20:07 187

tread

I tread
tred

II trod / treaded ★
trɒd / ˈtrɛdɪd ★

III trod / trodden / tread ★
trɒd / ˈtrɒdn / trɛd ★

To tread means to take steps (or walk) over, along, or onto something.

6 – 20:57 202

underwrite

I underwrite
ˌʌndəˈraɪt

II underwrote
ˌʌndəˈrəʊt

III underwritten
ˌʌndəˈrɪtn

To underwrite means to formally take on monetary risk (frequently connected to insurance) with an agreement to pay in the case of loss.

6 – 21:47 207

weep

I weep
wiːp

II wept
wept

III wept
wept

To weep means to release tears from the eyes (often connected to strong positive or negative emotions).

6 – 22:34 216

withstand

I withstand
wɪð'stænd, wɪθ'stænd

II withstood
wɪð'stʊd, wɪθ'stʊd

III withstood
wɪð'stʊd, wɪθ'stʊd

To withstand means to succeed in enduring or holding your position against something.

6 – 23:17 222

wring

I wring
rɪŋ

II wrung
rʌŋ

III wrung
rʌŋ

To wring means to cause liquid to be released from something (such as cloth) by applying pressure, often in a twisting motion.

6 – 24:00 223

INDEX

A

B

C

H

I

K

L

M

O

P

Q

R

S

T

U

W